ENGLISH *für* Germans

A fun look at English, especially for Germans.

by Simon Geraghty

If you are a German speaker and you want to learn English, this book can help. It can show you that you already know a lot. **Echt!**

In Germany you are surrounded by English - on radio, on TV, and online. Many English words are used in German - like *party*, *relax* and *bikini*. Some words are the same, e.g. *sex*.

So with the words you already know as a good basis, this book will help you to have fun learning and speaking English. Have fun!

Viel Spaß!

ISBN 978-1-4478-7476-8

Written, designed and
illustrated by Simon Geraghty.

www.EnglishfuerGermans.de

CONTENTS

I. BASICS

Ok, firstly: relax. It is ok to not speak perfect English. Really. If you live in Germany you have a head full of English already;

Bluejeans, high heels, Irish Pub...
...temporarily unavailable...
...the same procedure as every year...
....and last but not least... Happy End!

You hear English songs every day on the radio Maybe you have a few albums in English. This book will help - **die Lücke zu füllen** - where your English is missing. You will feel good about speaking English. Honestly.

If you look at it as a pain, it will be hard.

If you look at it as a game, it will be fun!

Here are some friendly words to get you started:

English	**German**
accent	Akzent
alphabet	Alphabet
baby	Baby
ball	Ball
camera	Kamera
format	Format
glass	Glas
golf	Golf
guarantee	Garantie
hamburger	Hamburger
hobby	Hobby
humor	Humor
man	Mann
maximum	Maximum
moment	Moment
optimist	Optimist
original	Original
poker	Poker
xylophone	Xylophon

These words are your friends. They will help...

Present Simple

In English there are two ways of talking about the present. The first way is talking about what happens all the time. For example:

Every day the optimist *smiles.*

In Scotland *it rains* all the time (or often).

Some more examples:
Usually *I work* every day.
You play poker every week.
We sleep every night.

So *I work, you play, we sleep, they party....* all the time.

The exceptions are “he”, “she” or “it”, which need “s” at the end of the word. For example; he work**s**, she play**s**, it happen**s** (all the time).

Even more examples:
The moon *shines,*
the girl *screams,*
the vampire *laughs...*

All the Time

(often, sometimes, on Sundays etc...)

I play:
- I play the guitar.
- I don't play golf.
- Do you play the xylophone?

He / She / It } plays tennis.

Does { He / She / It } play the piano?

He / She / It } doesn't play for Manchester United.

On the opposite page we have the positive, negative and question forms. Here it's *I play the guitar, I don't play golf* and *Do you play the xylophone?* It is just the same for 'you', 'we', and 'they'.

You (plural) like schnapps.
We don't drink hamburgers.
Do they enjoy whiskey?

This only changes with "he", "she" or "it"... You may remember from school:

he/she/it = das «S» muss mit!

He play**S**, she play**S**, it play**S**...

For example:
He love**S** her. She hate**S** him. It i**S** complicated.

'S' is also in the negative and question forms:

He doe**S**n't stop loving her.
She doe**S**n't like the situation.
Doe**S** it get better or worse..?

A LITTLE FOOTBALL STORY

NOT NOW, SOMETIMES...

I PLAY FOOTBALL ON SUNDAYS.
YOU WATCH THE GAMES.
IT RAINS MOST DAYS.
DO WE WIN THE GAMES?
WE WIN ONE IN TEN, AND
THEY ARE THE BEST GAMES .

{This story does not have the "you (plural)" form - see page 5}

So when do you use this? When you describe what happens *often* (I often visit Grandma), or what happens *all the time* (she always drinks tea) or *usually* (Grandpa sleeps in the afternoon), or *sometimes* (he forgets my name sometimes).

Do you speak Swahili?

I know a few words.

I don't practice often.

Do you understand the structure?

I hope the idea is clear.

We don't need to repeat it.

Remember:

he/she/it = das «S» muss mit!

Doe**S** it make sense?

The structure i**S** simple.

Practice make**S** perfect...

Anyway, back to the present. The other way of talking about the present is talking about now. So, at the moment, right now, you are reading, you are holding a book in your hands.

You are learning English.

It is getting easier.

We are making progress.

And that's how you say it;

I am,
you are,
he/she/it is,
we/you/they are...

...writing, listening, talking, laughing, partying.

And you can use this form when talking about **right now** or **at the moment**. (**gerade jetzt**). Let's look at more examples – right now, the sun is shining, the wind is blowing, the birds are singing, everybody is growing older. Are you smiling?

Right now,
this woman
is multi-tasking...

At the moment... she is shopping, texting, drinking coffee, smiling, and waving to a friend.

She is also eating chocolate. Is it snowing? No.

She is not sleeping, she is not learning Swahili, and she is not playing bass guitar in a jazz band.

Earth is not being attacked by aliens, right now.

Now, at the moment…

I am writing.

You are reading.

Is it getting clearer?

We are communicating.

Are you following these examples?

They are spelling out the structure for you...

Let's take a closer look at this...

This works with the verb 'to be':

I am
You are
he/she/it is
You (pl.)/we/they are... } + "-ing"

Right now, I am not punching the president, you are not performing a striptease. Is this making sense?

So, **at the moment, now**, you can say *I am* etc + *-ing* (e.g. you are reading). My dog is not singing. Is it becoming clearer?

ON THE OTHER HAND...

When you talk about **all the time** you can use the *simple* → She reads "Der Spiegel" *every week*, He looks at the photos in "Bild Zeitung" *every day*.

{TIP}

Is it happening "NOW" or not?

When should you say "I dance..."
and when should you say "I'm dancing..."?

The key is...

IS IT HAPPENING NOW?

→ NO → say...

"I dance (with Bob every Friday)"

→ YES → say...

"I'm dancing with Bob right now,
He is standing on my foot at the moment."

Some verbs **always** take the simple form (they're called "stative verbs"). Here are some of the more common examples:

I **understand**...

I **remember** this from school...

It **seems** to be quite simple...

I **wish** everything was this easy...

I **know** some things are harder...

I **hate** difficult things...

I **like** easy things...

I also **like** ice cream...

A LITTLE NIGHT CLUB STORY

NOW - IT'S 3am...

I AM DANCING.

YOU ARE SINGING.

IT IS GETTING VERY LATE.

ARE WE PARTYING TOO MUCH?

WE ARE TESTING THE WAITERS!

THEY ARE CALLING THE POLICE.

{This story doesn't have the "you (plural)" form - see p11}

A "Memory Hook" is a word or phrase that helps you remember something easily. In German you have the word "**Eselsbrücke**". This directly translates as "Donkey Bridge"!

For example, people can find these letters hard:

i and e   g and j   V and W

Memory hooks: **e**mail D**J** T**V** **i**Phone.

Are you emailing *right now*?

I am DJing *at the moment.*

I am not watching TV.

Are you paying attention?

I am trying to explain.

It is not going badly.

Remember:

you can use this to talk about now - or at the moment...

Is it sinking in?

It is becoming clearer.

We are making progress.

What **Hermann the German** says...

I ~~am liking~~ English. →

I'~~m knowing~~ it from school.

I'~~m not speaking~~ it often.

I'~~m not remembering~~ everything.

So I ~~am having~~ lessons every Monday.

At the moment, I ~~write~~ my homework...

...it ~~takes~~ a long time...

...and so my hand ~~gets~~ tired...

...so I ~~find~~ it hard.

Am ~~I practicing~~ English often?

Sometimes I'~~m visiting~~ the Irish Pub.

Usually I'~~m having~~ fun!

What **Hermann the German** should say...

I **like** English.

I **know** it from school.

I **do not speak** it *often.*

I **don't remember** everything.

So I **have** lessons *every Monday.*

....

At the moment, I **am writing** my homework...

...it **is taking** a long time...

...and so my hand **is getting** tired...

...so I **am finding** it hard.

....

Do I practice English *often*?

Sometimes **I visit** the Irish Pub.

Usually **I have** fun!

Part One – All the time

{TIP → use page 4 to help you...}

Create questions...

1. It normally rains during Wimbledon.

   e.g. Does it normally rain during Wimbledon?

2. Sometimes it rains all day long.

   ....

3. People often bring umbrellas.

   ....

4. They usually eat strawberries and cream.

   ....

5. Boris always attends the event.

   ....

6. An Englishman almost never wins Wimbledon.

   ....

Answers 2. Does it sometimes rain all day long? 3. Do people often bring umbrellas? 4. Do they usually eat strawberries and cream? 5. Does Boris always attend the event? 6. Does an Englishman ever win Wimbledon?

Part Two – At the moment

Right now, we are in London.

{TIP → use page 12 to help you...}

Create questions...

1. The sun is shining at Wimbledon today.

   e.g. Is the sun shining at Wimbledon today?

2. Boris and Steffi are eating strawberries.

   ....

3. An Englishman is playing on centre court.

   ....

4. He is not winning.

   ....

5. Now the clouds are arriving.

   ....

6. The people are putting up their umbrellas.

   ....

Answers *(...today...)* 2. Are Boris and Steffi eating strawberries? 3. Is an Englishman playing on centre court? 4. Is he winning? 5. Are the clouds are arriving *(now)*? 6. Are the people putting up their umbrellas?

Part Three - All the time *or* at the moment

Create negative sentences...

1. I understand.

e.g. I don't understand.

2. You are being helpful.

....

3. This method feels good.

....

4. I am improving my skills.

....

5. This book is bad.

....

Part Four - Help **Hermann**

Can you correct his mistakes?

a. My friend ~~have~~ a cool guitar. ____________

b. ~~He is playing~~ it every night. ____________

c. He ~~don't~~ play in a band. ____________

d. He ~~like~~ loud music. ____________

e. ~~Play you~~ the guitar? ____________

Answers Part Three 2. *You are not being helpful.* 3. *This method does not feel good.* 4. *I am not improving my skills.* 5. *This book is not bad.* Part 4 a. *...has...* b. *He plays...* c. *...doesn't play...* d. *...likes...* e. *Do you play..?*

II. HELP

If you still need help, this is the chapter for you. Here's the good news is - English is not as hard as you think. Learners of English in Germany often think you must know all of the grammar before you can speak. But is this really true?

What you actually need to speak the language is confidence (**Selbstvertrauen**). English is to be enjoyed, just like life. Luckily there are several easy ways to help remember words.

What they don't tell you in school is this... in real life nobody cares about your grammar - they just want to understand you. Understand?

Here are some more friendly words to help you:

English	**Deutsch**
active	aktiv
experiment	Experiment
fact	Fakt
favorite	Favorit
hammer	Hammer
idiot	Idiot
jargon	Jargon
logic	Logik
method	Methode
mild	mild
modern	modern
motor	Motor
museum	Museum
nature	Natur
object	Objekt
optimal	optimal
perfect	perfekt
video	Video

These words are your friends. They will help...

In English, we have different ways of talking about the past and the present. The first one is simple – I worked. For example – I worked in an Irish Pub in 1995. That's in the past, it's finished, it is over, **vorbei**, *finito*.

So you can use the verb (work) + – ed = "I worked". Franz Beckenbauer played for Germany many years ago – it's finished. You can use it any time you talk about the past that is finished like last month, yesterday, a year ago…

Last night I talked to my friend on the phone. He visited his Mum last week. They played poker. She started to win. So, he cooked dinner for her.

"This is the past, the *simple* past."

(Try reading that again in a James Bond voice).

It's simple. There are some words that are a bit special, but don't worry about that for now. Don't worry – be happy...

Finished Time

(it's over, completed, **vorbei**...)

We loved	We loved Abba.
	We didn't love Adam Ant.
	Did you love Alphaville?

I danced	I danced tango *yesterday*.
	I didn't dance chacha *last week*.
	Did we dance mambo *last year*?

Let's take a closer look at "Finished Time". On the oposite page you have the positive, negative and question forms. In this case it's...

We loved Abba.
We didn't love Adam Ant.
Did you love Alphaville?

All these bands played in the 1980s.
The 1980s are finished.

What songs did you love last year?

You can tell if it's finished by words like... yesterday, last week, last month or last year.

It's the same for time that is completed, such as, 8am yesterday, last Tuesday, October, 1960 etc.

Some examples of simple past...

...things that are finished:

yesterday

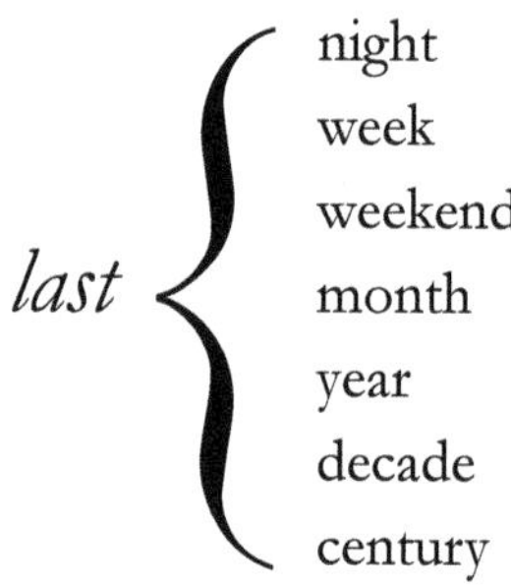

...your childhood...
...history...
...the dinosaurs etc.

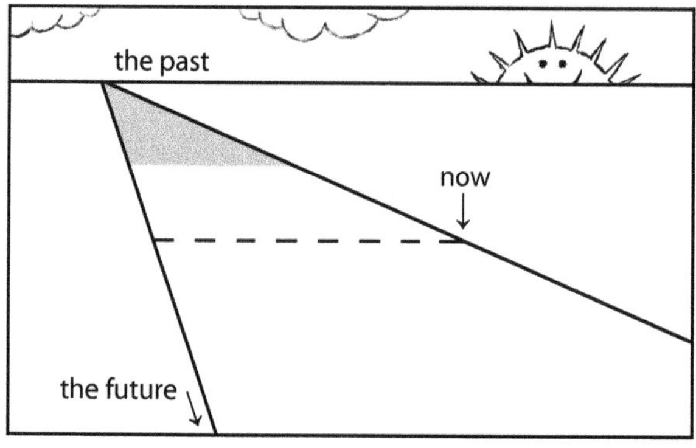

Did you fix your bike *last* weekend?

No, I didn't have time.

I surfed the internet.

Did you clean your room *yesterday*?

No, I waited for help.

I didn't want to do it alone.

Did you play computer games *last* night?

Yes, I finished every level!

I didn't sleep at all.

So, once again, when can you use this? If you're decribing something that is <u>finished</u>, over, past, **vorbei**. You probably covered this in school.

For example:
Yesterday I worked at home,
it rained, we cooked lasagne.

We use this form when we talk about the past. Like this:

I did not sleep all day.
It was not sunny.
We did not cook spaghetti.

Let's look at another main way of talking about the past and present. Remember the example of "I worked in an Irish Pub in 1995"? Let's say that you now work in a beergarden.

You have worked in a beergarden for two years (you still work there) i.e. IT'S NOT FINISHED.

In 1995 I worked in an Irish Pub – that is finished. It's over. Completed.

You have worked in a beergarden for two years – AND YOU STILL WORK THERE...

That is the key – **is it finished or not**?

I watched TV last night (it's finished). I have watched two DVDs this week (this week is not finished – I might watch three DVDs this week). *This* week is **un**finished, not over, (**nicht vorbei**).

Last week/month/year I watch*ed*/play*ed* etc...
This week/month/year I *have* watch*ed* etc...

Unfinished Time

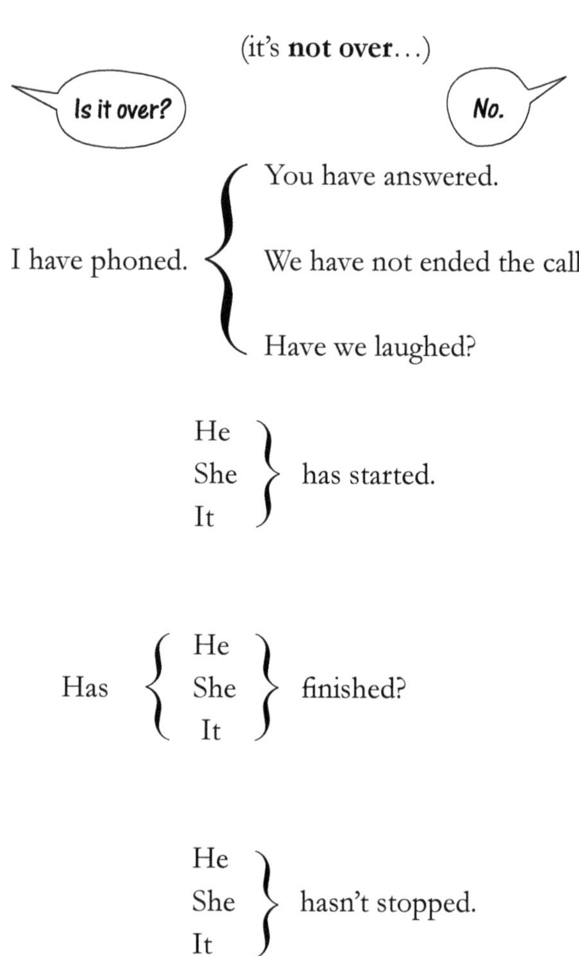

Let's take a closer look at this...

On the opposite page we have the form we use for **un**finished time. In this case the examples are:

I have phoned.
You have answered.
We have not ended the call.
Have we laughed?

Then we need "**s**" when we use **he**, **she** or **it**...

*He ha***s** / *she ha***s** / *it ha***s** *started...*

The negative and question forms also have "**s**"

*Ha***s** *it finished?*
*It ha***s***n't finished.*

This is the important part:
The situation is **un**finished,
therefore we use *have* or *ha***s** (+ verb).

This deals with the present (**un**finished). That is important - it's a present tense. You can use it to describe the recent past, or what still affects the present...

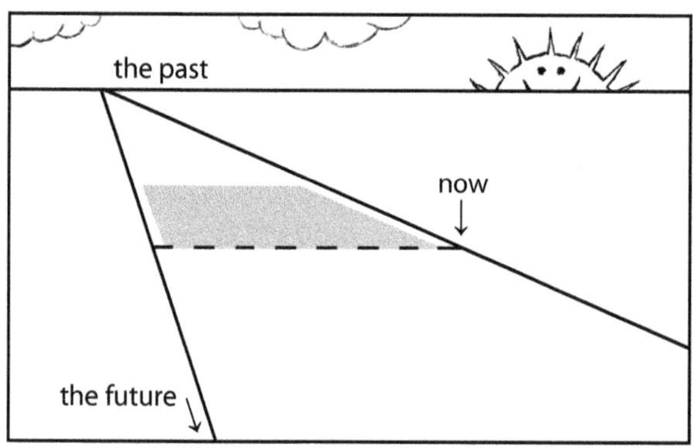

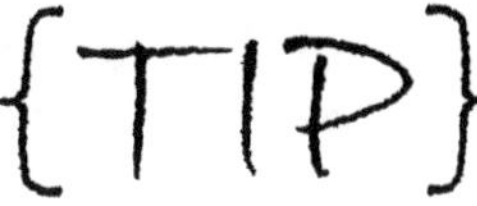

These things that are **un**finished:

this { week / month / year, etc...

Have you killed anybody *this year*?

I haven't kicked anybody *this month.*

I have kissed somebody *this week.*

Has John washed *this year*?

He has showered *this month.*

But he hasn't washed *this week.*

Have they enjoyed *this year*?

They have laughed *this month.*

But they haven't smiled *this week...*

Special Words

Some words in English are special, such as:

"To drive"

Today - I **drive**
Yesterday - I **drove**
This week - I have **driven**

These special words have three forms.

The first form is the infinitve (drive), the second is used for finished time (drove), and the third for **un**finished time (driven).

{This third form uses "have" or "has" (+ verb)}

It might help to think of these forms as

one two three

drive drove driven

We'll come back to that later. Here you can see some of most typical special words...

one	two	three
break	broke	broken
choose	chose	chosen
speak	spoke	spoken
write	wrote	written
eat	ate	eaten
fall	fell	fallen
forget	forgot	forgotten
give	gave	given
see	saw	seen
take	took	taken
know	knew	known
fly	flew	flown
begin	began	begun
drink	drank	drunk
swim	swam	swum
sing	sang	sung
run	ran	run
come	came	come
become	became	become

Some of the special words are exactly the same in form two and three, for example:

one	two	three
send	sent	sent
spend	spent	spent
lose	lost	lost
get	got	got
sit	sat	sat
leave	left	left
meet	met	met
bring	brought	brought
buy	bought	bought
think	thought	thought
teach	taught	taught
sell	sold	sold
tell	told	told
find	found	found
have	had	had
hear	heard	heard
read	read*	read*
say	said	said
pay	paid	paid
make	made	made
stand	stood	stood
understand	understood	understood

** pronounced [red]*

Some special words do not change at all:

one	**two**	**three**
cost	cost	cost
cut	cut	cut
hit	hit	hit
hurt	hurt	hurt
let	let	let
put	put	put
shut	shut	shut

How can you use this? *[1. fly 2. flew 3. flown]*

one for finished negative: I didn't fly...
and finished question: Did I fly...?

two for finished positive: I flew...

three for **un**finished negative: I haven't flown...
question: Have I flown...?
and positive: I have flown...

[For a full list of special words google "irregular English verbs"]

What Hermann the German says...

Last year I'~~ve visited~~ Italy. →

This year I ~~didn't have~~ a holiday yet.

So I ~~choose~~ a new option last week...

...a Greek hotel ~~catched~~ my attention online.

I ~~send~~ an email to them last Monday.

At 9am on Tuesday they ~~have called~~ me...

...the Greek lady ~~has sounded~~ friendly.

We ~~have had~~ a nice chat for 15 minutes...

...and I ~~have decided~~ to book a room.

The next day I ~~have flown~~ to Greece.

The sun ~~has shined~~ every day ~~I've been~~ there...

...and I ~~have eaten~~ Greek food every evening.

It was the best holiday I ever ~~have~~.

What **Hermann the German** should say...

Last year I **visited** Italy.

This year I **haven't had** a holiday *yet.*

So I **chose** a new option *last week*...

...a Greek hotel **caught** my attention online.

I **sent** an email to them *last Monday.*

At *9am on Tuesday* they **called** me...

...the Greek lady **sounded** friendly...

...we **had** a nice chat for 15 minutes...

...and I **decided** to book a room.

The next day I **flew** to Greece.

The sun **shone** *every day I* **was** *there*...

...and I **ate** Greek food *every evening.*

It was the best holiday I **have ever had**.

Part One – The Past {TIP → use page 28...}

It's 9pm on Friday. Make sentences to complete the story.

1. Everybody / be busy / at work last week

   e.g. Everybody was busy at work last week.

2. We / forget / Phil's birthday / on Monday

   ....

3. So I / buy/ a nice gift / yesterday

   ....

4. We / leave it on his desk / at 9.00am

   ....

5. Phil / find the card / at 2pm

   ....

6. The boss / give Phil / a hug at 5.00pm

   ....

7. We / go / to the pub after work

   ....

Answers 2. We *forgot* Phil's birthday on Monday. 3. So I *bought* a nice gift yesterday. 4. We *left* it on his desk at 9.00am. 5. Phil *found* the card at 2pm. 6. The boss *gave* Phil a hug at 5.00pm. 7. We *went* to the Pub after work!

Part Two – Special Words {TIP → use page 39...}

Tell the story with the correct form of the right word.

fly	get	write	speak	have	read
meet	choose	spend	know	begin	fall

1. Have you ever …….……… in love suddenly?

2. I've only …….……… Pat for a week.

3. We …….……… back from Paris yesterday.

4. We …….……… at a business meeting last month.

5. Pat …….……… me an email the next day.

6. We …….……… to mail each other every few minutes.

7. We …….……… to visit Paris for work on Monday.

8. We …….……… the whole week together.

9. We …….……… engaged to be married yesterday...

10. ...and we …….……… Las Vegas for our wedding.

Answers 1. fallen 2. known. 3. flew. 4. met. 5. wrote.
6. began. 7. had. 8. spent. 9. engaged. 10. chose.

Part Three – Questions {TIP → use page 34...}

{finished or **UN**finished}

Create questions.

1. Yes, I've heard the news.

   Have you heard the news?

2. He drove to Budapest.

   ………………………………………

3. She flew to Bucharest.

   ………………………………………

4. They haven't spoken to each other yet.

   ………………………………………

5. Yes, they've both gone to the wrong city.

   ………………………………………

   (Explanation: They both should have gone to Bratislava)

Answers 2. Did he drive to Budapest? 3. Did she fly to Bucharest? 4. Have they spoken to each other? 5. Have they both gone to the wrong city?

III. WORK

Good Business English is not complicated. It's simple. If you get the basic words you'll be fine. With all aspects of English there are some essential words. If you know these terms and work with them, you shouldn't have too many problems. Practice is the key.

"Learning by doing" is a great way to make progress. You are always learning... (and it helps if you are getting paid while you learn).

Don't be afraid to ask English-speaking colleagues to correct you. Or better still, go to the Irish Pub with them. Communication is the most important thing. It's good to use simple words. And short sentences.

Here are some more friendly words to help you:

English	**Deutsch**
bank	Bank
complex	komplex
computer	Computer
design	Design
discussion	Diskussion
effective	effektiv
global	global
industry	Industrie
international	International
job	Job
list	Liste
machine	Maschine
manager	Manager
million	Million
motto	Motto
organisation	Organisation
permanent	permanent

Think of these words as helpful colleagues...

{TIP → say "col*league*" - like Champion's *League*...}

In English we don't have "**Sie**" and "**du**", but we are overly polite. ☺ In business it is good to use soft phrases like these:

Could... and Would...

...for requests:

"Could you find the report?"
"Would you like me to deliver it?"

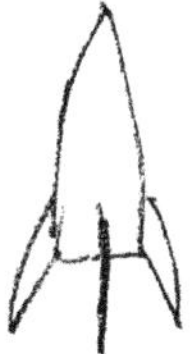

I'm afraid...

...for any negative information:

"I'm afraid I lost the report...
and I'm afraid I crashed the car."
"I'm afraid you're fired."

might & slight...

...for nuance:

"That might be a slight (**kleines**) problem.."

Future 1 - "Will"

(facts, beliefs, decisions, etc…)

I will have a party.

You will enjoy it.

It will be great.

What will we eat?

We will have sandwiches.

They will taste great.

They will not last long.

[*will not = won't*]

We use the "Will" future to talk about...

...things we see as facts...

The winter will be cold.

Liechtenstein will not win the World Cup.

...or beliefs...

He will go to hell when he dies.

She will go to heaven when she dies.

...or instant decisions...

I'll sing a song.

I'll kick your ass.

...etc...

Meet Rod, Al and Sid.

Remember their names.

They're going to help you with business words.

Rod works in product development.

Al works on system analysis.

Sid works in a subsidiary. Filiale

(Try saying the underlined *parts just like the names.)*

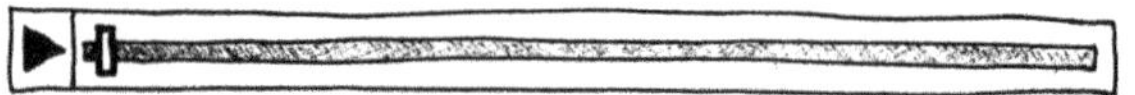

[Listen to an audio version of this on www.EnglishfuerGermans.de]

Ask your friends or colleagues to correct your mistakes. It costs nothing to ask...

By the way, here are some English words that are often used in German business situations:

Business as usual
normaler Betrieb

Headhunter
Abwerber

Laptop
Klapprechner

Management
Betriebsleitung

Marketing
Absatzwirtschaft

Meeting
Besprechung

Outsourcing
Externbeschaffung

Upgrade
Aufrüstung

Workflow
Abläufe

Workshop
Arbeitsseminar

THE DIFFERENCE BETWEEN: *THIS & THAT + HERE & THERE*

Let's imagine that we are in an Irish Pub now, sitting at a long table...

I am **here**.	You are **there**.
This is my beer.	That is your beer.
This is my whiskey.	That's your schnapps.
These, **here**,	Those, **there**,
are my drinks.	are your drinks.

Cheers! **Prost!**

TELPHONE HELP

When you make a phone call in English the most important thing is to stay calm - keep breathing! If you don't understand something, don't panic, try using some of these phrases and questions:

I didn't catch that.

Sorry, what was that?

Could you repeat that please?

Would you mind speaking slowly, please?

I'm not sure I'm with you, do you mean...?

OK, that's everything from my side.

Thanks very much. Goodbye.

BUSINESS WRITING TIP

Countries, Languages and Nationalities are ALWAYS capitalised, for example:

The British manager of the South American office doesn't speak Spanish.

Acronyms Challenge

You are starting a new job in London as a PA. On your CV it said you were fluent in spoken and written English. On your first day you get a message from your boss, marked "urgent"...

```
Title: FYI

Hi, Tomorrow we've two VIPs coming:
the USA CEO and the EU CFO.
They're visiting HQ to inspect
the IT, PR, HR and R&D departments.
So we need an FAQ a.s.a.p. Thanks, B.

P.S. The CFO likes to talk about GDP,
so we better include that in the FAQ.
```

What do each of the acronyms stand for..?

PA Personal Assistant
CV Curriculum Vitae
FYI For Your Information
VIP Very Important Person
UK United Kingdom
USA United States of America
CEO Chief Executive Officer
EU European Union
CFO Chief Financial Officer
HQ Headquarters
IT Information Technology
PR Public Relations
HR Human Resources
R&D Research and Development
FAQ Frequently Asked Questions
a.s.a.p. as soon as possible
P.S. Post Script
GDP Gross Domestic Product

"...talking B.S."

While watching an American news channel you might hear a journalist say the following:

"I'm afraid the Senator is talking B.S."

It is important that students of English understand what this sentence means.

Don't think that - in this context - B.S. stands for Business Studies.

Maybe you can guess what it stands for...

Future 2 - "Going to"

(plans, predictions etc)

I am going to explain this idea.

You are going to understand.

It is going to be pretty easy.

We are going to enjoy the examples.

They are going to make you smile*!

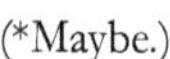

We use "going to" when we talk about...

...plans...

He is going to kill his wife.

She is going to murder her husband.

They are going to leave the country.

...or predictions...

It is going to be a disaster.

He is going to get caught.

They are going to go to prison.

DON'T WORRY!

Sometimes you can use " will" OR "going to",

for example - *"I am going to hug Mum."*

You can see this as a plan.

"I will hug Mum when I see her."

You can see this as a fact.

DON'T WORRY!

The main thing to remember is:
"will"= facts/beliefs/decisions
"going to" = plans/predictions

[for more information google "English future tenses"]

In general, Business in the English-speaking world is more relaxed than in Germany. So you and your boss could be on first name terms.

However, this also means that you need to be “hip”, “with-it”, “streetwise”, etc...

...It’s important not to come across as boring. One of the big differences between the two cultures is humour.

For instance, generally speaking in Germany if somebody uses too much humour in a business presentation they might not be taken seriously.

In English-speaking business culture, if you don’t use at least a little bit of humour you may be considered dull and boring (langweilig).

So lighten up and have some fun!

übrigens

By the way...

If you want an example of how many English words you can find in Germany every day, look in a supermarket, and you'll see words like these:

New
Super
Active
Plus
Fresh
Classic
Extra
Deluxe
Instant
Pocket
Original
Balance
High Grade
King Size
Sugar Free
Great Value
Hot Chili
Exotic Sauce
Cheese Dip
Barbeque
For Men

And then take a stroll into the part of the supermarket dedicated to products for women and you'll find lots of lovely words like these:

Pure
Cream
Honey
Energy
Natural
Herbal
Delight
Vitality
Wash
Styling
Highlights
Sensitive
Super Soft
Bath Care
Deep Black
Rich Brown
Sunny Blonde
Body & Hair
Brilliance
Hands & Nails
Excellence

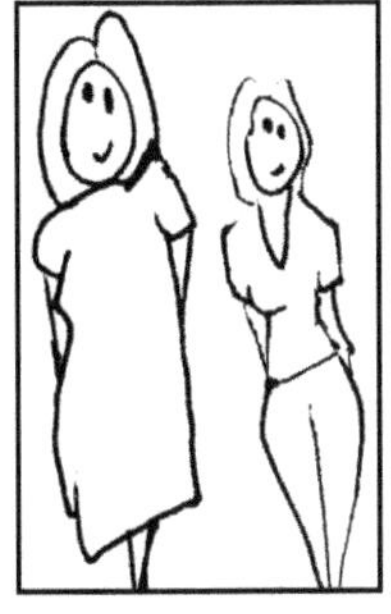

False Friends

Watch out for these "false friend" words...

English word	**German**	**False Friend**	***Correct***
actual	wirklich	~~aktuell~~	*latest*
caution	Vorsicht	~~Kaution~~	*deposit*
consequent	folgend	~~konsequent~~	*consistent*
failure	Misserfolg	~~Fehler~~	*mistake*
guilty	schuldig	~~gültig~~	*valid*
meaning	Bedeutung	~~Meinung~~	*opinion*
rent	mieten	~~Rente~~	*pension*
sensible	vernünftig	~~sensibel~~	*sensitive*
serious	ernst	~~seriös~~	*respectable*
to become	werden	~~bekommen~~	*to get*
sea	Meer	~~See~~	*lake*
where	wo	~~wer~~	*who*
while	während	~~weil~~	*because, as*
who	wer	~~wo~~	*where*
I will	ich werde	~~ich will~~	*I want**

*It's better to say "I would like" than "I want".

Your colleague Brian Smith, who is a mutual acquaintance, gave me your contact details.	→	I got your details from Brian Smith.
It would be great if you could take a moment to read through this file.	→	Could you please check this document?
I would very much appreciate your help with this document.	→	I hope you can help.
If you could do this for me I'd be extremely happy.	→	Thank you in advance.
{This is well written, but too long}		*{This gets to the point}*

What **Hermann the German** says...

...in presentations...

I would like to ~~present you~~ my report. →

I'~~m starting~~ off with a look at the market...

Have a look ~~to~~ the chart…

~~That's it!~~

...on the phone...

~~Here is Hermann.~~

~~Who are you?~~

~~What do you want?~~

~~Until I hear you again...~~

...in meetings...

~~I don't understand you. My English is so bad!~~

I'd like to say something ~~to~~ the topic.

~~You are wrong!~~

~~What?~~

...in emails...

~~HELLO DAVE!!!~~

I need ~~these informations RIGHT NOW!!!!~~

The price is ~~21.000,00 $~~.

~~Greetings~~, Hermann.

What **Hermann the German** should say...

I would like to **present you with** my report.
I'll start off with a look at the market...
Have a look **at** the chart…
Thank you for your attention.

Hermann speaking. / This is Hermann.
May I ask who is calling, please?
How can I help you?
Goodbye.

I'm not sure I'm with you.
I'd like to say something **about** the topic.
I'm afraid I disagree.
Pardon?

Hi Dave,
I need **this information as soon as possible**.
The price is **$21,000.00.**
Best regards, Hermann.

Part One – Future 1 - "Will"

{TIP → use page 52 to help you...}

Create sentences with "will"...

1. Adam / kiss / Steve

   e.g. Adam will kiss Steve.

2. Steve / kick / Adam

   ....

3. Adam / punch / Steve

   ....

4. Steve / cry

   ....

5. Adam / laugh

   ....

6. Steve / go / to the hospital

   ....

Answers 2. Steve will kick Adam. 3. Adam will punch Steve. 4. Steve will cry. 5. Adam will laugh. 6. Steve will go to the hospital.

Part Two – Future 2 - "Going to"

Right now, we are in London.

{TIP → use page 60 to help you...}

Create sentences with "going to"...

1. I / fly / to London / on Friday

   e.g. I'm going to fly to London on Friday.

2. I / attend / a business meeting

   ....

3. I / go / shopping / on Saturday

   ....

4. I / visit / Wembley Stadium

   ....

5. I / have / a great time

   ....

6. I / be / tired / on Monday

   ....

Answers 2. I'm going to attend a business meeting. 3. I'm going to go shopping. 4. I'm going to visit Wembley Stadium. 5. I'm going to have a great time. 6. I'm going to be very tired.

Part Three - "Will" or "Going to"

Create sentences... {TIP → use page 62 to help you...}

1.PLAN: Bob / have / a party

....

2. FACT: It / take place / Saturday

....

3. PREDICTION: It / be / full of people

....

4. BELIEF: I hope / Bob / have / enough beer

....

5. DECISION: I / buy /extra beer

....

Part Four - Help Hermann *Can you correct his mistakes?*

a. PLAN: I ~~go~~ to Bob's party on Friday. ____________

b. FACT: ~~It gives~~ lots of girls there. ____________

c. PREDICTION: It ~~makes~~ fun. ____________

d. BELIEF: I hope Bob ~~have~~ music. ____________

e. DECISION: I ~~bring~~ my accordian. ____________

Answers Part Three 1. Bob is going to have a party. 2. It will take place on Saturday. 3. It is going to be full of people. 4. I hope Bob will have enough people. 5. I will buy extra beer. Part Four a. *...am going to go...* b. *There will be...* c. *...is going to be...* d. *...will have...* e. *...will bring...*

IV. PLAY

English can be child's play, if you can enjoy learning it. The whole world speaks English, so the world opens up to you when you do...

There are a lot of fun things to do with the English language. Going to an Irish Pub is just one. Most cities in Germany have at least one Irish Pub and quite often the customers are international English speakers. Another fun place for English is the Internet – it's very big, and full of English stories, movies, radio stations etc.

Learning English is a game that you can't lose. And you can play it for the rest of your life. Now that you know the most important rules, it's time to enjoy playing the game.

Playing the game can be child's play...

English	**Deutsch**
affair	Affäre
alcohol	Alkohol
band	Band (music)
beer	Bier
<u>con</u>cert	Konzert
cre<u>a</u>tive	kreativ
disco	Disko
entertainer	Entertainer
fiasco	Fiasko
grill	Grill
guitar	Gitarre
<u>lit</u>erature	Literatur
<u>mel</u>ancholy	Melancholie
melody	Melodie
film	Film
monster	Monster
<u>mu</u>sic	Musik
picnic	Picknick
rucksack	Rucksack

Think of these words as your playmates...

A FILM...

The creative monster played guitar in a band. He liked alcohol and he didn't like literature. He played music without melody. He was not an entertainer. He had beer in his rucksack, but he didn't have a picnic. His concert at the disco was a fiasco. After the whole affair the monster felt some melancholy. THE END.

Urban Legend*

Former German Chancellor Helmut Kohl wanted to tell US President Ronald Reagan that they could address each other informally, so he said to him "You can say 'you' to me".

{du kannst mich duzen}

* moderne Legende

IF 1

(likely, probably, **wahrscheinlich**)

If **you understand** this...
[present]

...the next part **will be** easy.
[future]

If **you pay** attention...
[present]

...I **will explain**...
[future]

When a situation is likely, we use

[If] + [the present]...

If I dance....

+ *[the future]*

...you will laugh!

If you don't understand...

...I will give you more examples.

If you read all of this book...

...your English will get better.

If your English gets better...

...you will enjoy your life more.

A LITTLE MURDER STORY

IF I DO... I WILL...

IF I SEE BILL… I WILL KILL HIM.
IF I KILL BILL… I WILL RUN AWAY.
IF I RUN AWAY… I WILL BE 'WANTED'!

I WON'T BE 'WANTED'... IF I DON'T KILL BILL.
I'LL CHANGE MY MIND... IF I THINK ABOUT IT…

wie bereits erwähnt

As previously mentioned...

If you think of English as a pain...

...it will be hard.

If you think of it as a game...

...it will be fun!

If you read this book...

...your English will improve.

If your English improves...

...you will feel great!

THE DIFFERENCE BETWEEN...

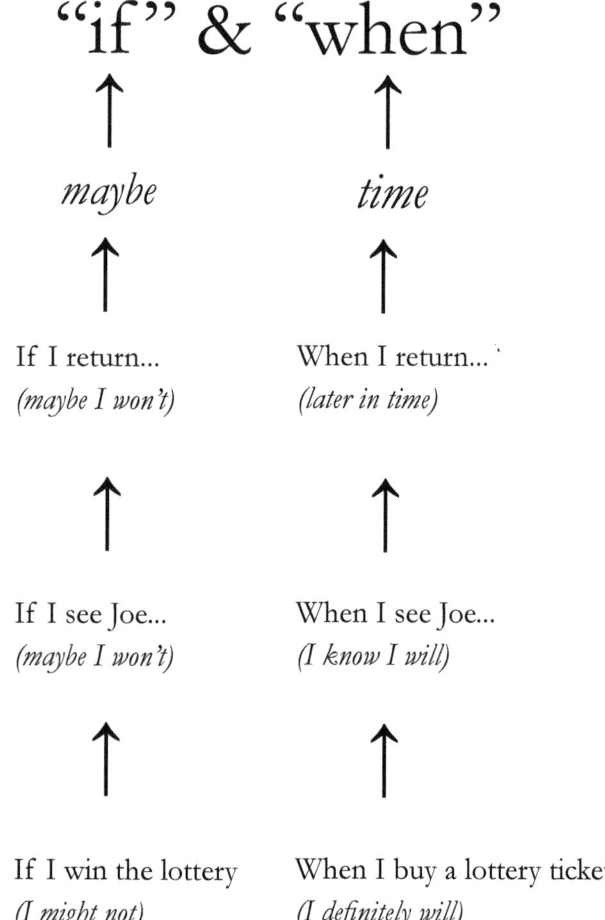

Incidentally (by the way)...

Most people know that a "handy"in English is a *mobile* or *cell phone*. Here are some more words that you might think are correct English, but really have a different meaning. On the right you can see the correct English word.

German usage	Correct English
Handy	mobile (UK) or cell phone (US)
Smoking	tuxedo →
Mobbing	bullying
Showmaster	host
Beamer	projector
Slip	knickers (UK) or panties (U.
Oldtimer*	vintage or classic car

*In English an *Oldtimer* is an old man

TO LEND OR TO BORROW?

to lend = to give (**ausleihen**)

to borrow = to take (**verleihen**)

For example, when you get a loan from a bank, they give (lend) and you take (borrow) money. The bank is a lender. You are a borrower.

One way to remember this is:

When you borr**ow**...

...you **ow**e somebody money.

When you l**end**...

...they sp**end** your money.

BUSINESS TIP

Try saying these business words using the tips:

Percent	like 50 cent
Executive	like “Sektglas”
Personnel	like “Schnell”
Target	like “Argument”

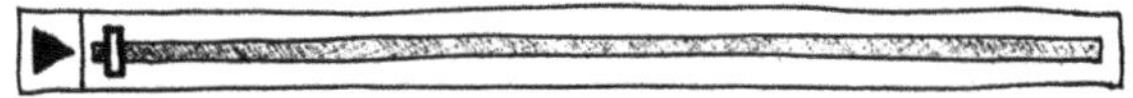

[Listen to an audio version of this on www.EnglishfuerGermans.de]

IF 2

(unlikely, improbable, **unwahrscheinlich**)

If **you kissed** an angel...
[past]

...it **would feel** heavenly.
[would]

If **you hugged** a hedgehog...
[past]

...it **would hurt**.
[would]

If **you killed** a kitten...
[past]

...you **would be** a criminal.
[would]

If a situation is unlikely, or improbable, we use

[If] + [the past]...

If the kitten was dead.... 

+ *[would/ could/ should]*

...it would feel nothing.

If nobody saw what happened...

...you could keep it a secret.

Would you keep it a secret...

...if nobody saw what happened?

If you killed a kitten...

...you should <u>not</u> keep it a secret!

THE DIFFERENCE BETWEEN...

[*You can use* for + since *for* **un**finished *situations.*]

In English you can use the word "much" to talk about uncountable things, for example:

There isn't much tourism.
Was there much traffic?
I won't have much energy.

And use "many" for countable things, e.g.

There aren't many tourists.
Were there many cars?
We won't have many problems...

BUT THE GOOD NEWS IS...

you can ALWAYS use

"a lot of"

There were a lot of tourists.
Was there a lot of traffic?
You won't have a lot of problems.

[*They don't tell you this in school!*]

Hermann is talking to an English tourist. It's her first time in Germany and it's his first time speaking English since school. They're in a bar beside his office and he wants to make small talk. An older man enters and says "**Guten Abend**".

Hermann says "**Ah, zat man is my chef**".

The English tourist. says,
"WOW, YOU HAVE YOUR OWN CHEF!"

. . . .

The next morning the English tourist says,
"So is your chef going to make us breakfast?"

Hermann says...

"**Ah... I sink ve haf a missuntterstandtink!**"

EXPLANATION: WHEN HE SAYS "CHEF" SHE THINKS HE MEANS "KÜCHENCHEF".

A LITTLE HOLIDAY STORY

<u>IF I DID... I WOULD...</u>

IF I WENT TO NEW YORK… I'D VISIT MIKE.
IF MIKE HAD TIME… WE'D SEE THE YANKEES.
IF THEY WON... WE WOULD CELEBRATE!
IF THEY DIDN'T WIN... WE'D COMMISERATE...

IF I HAD A HAMMER

I'D HAMMER IN THE MORNIN'!...

German *in* English

HOW MANY GERMAN WORDS CAN YOU FIND..?

The German-American man had wanderlust as a result of the zeitgeist. In his rucksack he had muesli, pumpernickel, sauerkraut and pilsner. He had angst because of a rottweiler he met in kindergarten, which was now “kaputt”.

The German-American had schadenfreude.

ANSWER: TWELVE.

What Hermann the German says...

I need to buy a new shirt ~~until~~ Saturday. ⟶

Should I ~~expain you the situation~~?

My neighbour is ~~extreme~~ pretty.

She looks ~~as~~ a super model.

She has lived next door ~~since~~ two years. ☺

She has a ~~good~~ designed behind.

I would like ~~her to know learn.~~

Yesterday I ~~meet~~ her on the street.

She ~~told~~ that she was single.

That's ~~the reason to buy~~ a new shirt.

~~On Saturday is another neighbour's party~~.

If the pretty girl comes, ~~I ask~~ her to dance.

If she ~~don't~~ come...

...~~I still have~~ a new shirt!

What **Hermann the German** should say...

I need to buy a new shirt *by* Saturday.

Should I *explain the situation to you?*

My neighbour is *extremely* pretty.

She looks *like* a super model.

She has lived next door *for* two years.

☺

She has a *well* designed behind.

I would like *to get to know her.*

Yesterday I *met* her in the street.

She *told me* that she was single.

That's *the reason I want to buy* a new shirt.

Another neighbour's party is on Saturday.

If the pretty girl comes, *I will ask* her to dance.

If she *doesn't* come...

...*I'll still have* a new shirt!

Part One – IF... {TIP → use pages 76 and 84...}

Tell the story with the correct form of the right word.

change	have	take	want	say	
look	think	ask	find	fall	be

Hermann hopes...

1. If he meets a nice girl tonight...

...he will .... her to go out with him.

2. If she .... yes...

...he will .... her out on the town.

3. He will .... really happy....

...if they .... in love..

Answers: 1. If he meets... he will ask... 2. If she says yes... he will take... 3. He will be really happy.... if they fall in love.

4. If he .... a girlfriend

....it would .... his life.

5. If she .... good...

...girls would .... him cool.

6. He wouldn't .... only one girlfriend...

...if girls .... he was cool.

Part Two – More Small Words...

Which correct small word should be used below?

a. Sarah bought a dress ~~in~~ the internet. ....

b. It wasn't ~~to~~ expensive. ....

c. It was cheaper ~~as~~ in the shops. ....

d. She is proud ~~on~~ herself ....

Answers: 4. If he had.... it would change... 5. If she looked... girls would find... 6. He wouldn't want... if girls thought...
Part Two: a. on, b.too, c. than, d. of.

Part Three – Song Titles

Hermann needs help...

He is trying to remember words from famous songs. Can you help by giving him the right words...

1. ~~It gives~~ a house in New Orleans. ....

2. Let's twist again ~~as~~ we did last summer ....

3. I'm dreaming ~~from~~ a white Christmas. ....

4. Welcome ~~by~~ the Hotel California. ....

5. She's ~~spying~~ a stairway to heaven. ....

6. Always look on the bright side of ~~live~~. ....

Answers: 1. *There is* a house in New Orleans. 2. Let's twist again *like* we did last summer. 3. I'm dreaming *of* a white Christmas. 4. Welcome *to* the hotel California. 5. *She's buying* a stairway to heaven. 6. Always look on the bright side of *life*.

V. FUN

Life is too short to not have a good time, right? So enjoy using the English language - sing along to your favourite song in the shower, badly. Don't take yourself too seriously, and don't take the English language too seriously.

And don't take the last sentence too seriously. It's all just a good laugh!

Life should be fun and learning should be fun, so have fun!

Here are some fun words to get you started:

English	**Deutsch**
anarchy	Anarchie
bikini	Bikini
blonde	blond
clown	Clown
club	Club
cocktail	Cocktail
fabulous	fabulös
fantastic	fantastisch
flirt	Flirt
gag	Gag
gorilla	Gorilla
hysterical	hysterisch
mango	Mango
massage	Massage
nipple	Nippel
nudist	Nudist
party	Party
peanuts	Peanuts

Think of these words as things to have fun with...

New Year's Eve in New York!

The blond in the bikini flirted with the clown. "People say my nipple massage is fantastic... I learnt it at a nudist party."

The clown laughed and bought her some peanuts and a mango cocktail, which tasted fabulous. Later they went to a club. The dancefloor was anarchy. A guy in a gorilla costume was getting hysterical. So they said "Auf Wiedersehen"!

"Same procedure as every year..."

Believe it or not, English-speaking people outside Germany do not know "Dinner for One". It is a German phenomenon. German TV first showed it in the 1960s, it was a big hit and now it is always played on New Year's Eve. But English-speaking people don't know it. So it quite often happens that German people will say to English-speaking people "Same procedure as every year - ha ha!". But we have no idea what you're talking about!

U.S. v U.K.

HOME	trashcan	dustbin	Mülleimer
	bathrooom	loo	Toilette
	sidewalk	footpath	Gehweg
FOOD	cotton candy	candyfloss	Zuckerwatte
	potatoe chips	crisps	Kartoffelchips
	dessert	pudding	Nachtisch
CLOTHES	sweater	jumper	Pullover
	pants	trousers	Hosen
	braces	suspenders	Hosenträger/ Strumpfhalter
CARS	hood	bonnet	Haube
	trunk	boot	Kofferraum
	gasoline	petrol	Benzin
SPELLING	color	colour	Farbe
	center	centre	Zentrum/Mitte
	to organize	to organise	organisieren
LIFE	kick the bucket	pop your clogs	abkratzen / den Löffel abgeben

Small Words

The smallest words in the English language:

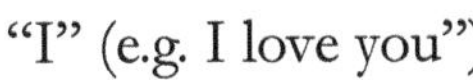

"I" (e.g. I love you")

and "a" (e.g. a kiss).

"a" is used for everything - almost...

"an" is used for words that start with

a → an angel

e → an e-mail

i → an igloo

o → an opera

u → an update

Some words start with "u" but sound like "y", like "uniform" or "unicorn" - so you use "a" .

All together: *I saw an opera where an angel sent an update in an e-mail from an igloo with a unicorn.*

Latin in English

There is also quite a bit of Latin in English:

ad hoc	improvised
bona fide	genuine
carpe diem	seize the day
curriculum vitae	résumé
etc (et cetera)	and so on
terra firma	solid land
vice versa	the other way around
*status quo**	current situation

* = *also a rock band*

French vis-à-vis English

You can use a lot of French words in English, here are just a few:

French	English
Bon appetit!	Enjoy your meal!
C'est la vie!	That's life!
Cliché	stereotype
Cul-de-sac	dead-end street
Décor	interior decoration
Faux pas	social blunder
Genre	type or class
Verve	flamboyance
Raconteur	conversationalist

The "th" sound

The "th" thing is a theme that's tricky.
Yet thankfully it's therapeutic. In theory.
Therefore try practicing slowly.
Put your tongue against your
teeth and theatrically say...

"...this, that, these and those..."

then this:

"...through thick 'n' thin...
...think thoughtfully..."

What's the smallest "th" sound?

That's a good question! The answer is the "th" sound in the word "clothes". It's very similar to the word "to close", but has a tiny "th" sound.

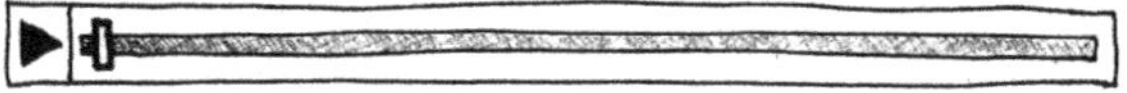

[Listen to an audio version of this on www.EnglishfuerGermans.de]

Quick Quiz

1. Can you ....?

    a. ...this question answer

    b. ...answer question this

    c. ...answer this question

2. This will ....

    a. only take a minute

    b. only a minute take

    c. a minute take only

3. This ....

    a. really is quite easy

    b. quite easy really is

    c. is quite really easy

4. Learning English ....

    a. can a lot of fun be

    b. a lot of fun can be

    c. can be a lot of fun

ANSWERS: 1. (c), 2. (a), 3. (b), 4. (d). *Ha ha - only joking!* **(c).**

Adverbs

If you're describing a verb (do, go, be, etc) nine times out of ten you'll need [- ***ly***]

For example:

He sings bad***ly***

She screams loud***ly***

The song ends sudden***ly***

They embrace passionate***ly***

The night ends beautiful***ly***

You understand complete***ly***, right?

IMPORTANT: THIS IS DIFFERENT TO GERMAN

GOOD NEWS!

With regard to adverbs,
there are only three main exceptions:

good → well

fast → fast

hard → hard

{*hardly* = **kaum**}

"DON'T MENTION THE WAR!" *You need to know this...*

In the 1970s in Britain there was a very popular TV show about a crazy hotel owner called Fawlty Towers. One of the best episodes was when some Germans come to stay. Basil, the owner, gets hit on the head and is even crazier than usual. He tells everybody to be careful in front of the Germans, and he keeps repeating "Don't mention the war!". But he talks about the war and Hitler, and chaos ensues... it's very funny. But the important thing for you to know is this: if you - as a German - say "don't mention the war" - people will probably find it funny.

PUB

A Guide to Irish Pubs

Be friendly... it helps!
Go ahead and speak English.

Don't be shy...
give it a try!

If you can talk you can sing!
If you can sing you can dance!

On 17th March it's
St. Patrick's Day
...so wear something green!

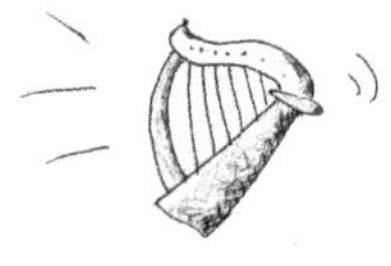

Here's a challenge: use one of the following prefixes to create the opposite of these words:

un...	im...	in...	mis...	ir...

.........polite
.........patient
.........possible
.........capable
.........friendly
.........efficient
.........responsible
........understand

Tongue Twisters

Challenging your powers of pronunciation...

She sells sea shells on the seashore of Seychelles.

Fred fed Ted bread, and Ted fed Fred bread.

He had "had". Had he had "had had", he'd have passed the examination.

Rory the warrior and Roger the worrier were reared wrongly in a rural brewery, weirdly.

Three witches watch three Swatch watches. Which witch watches which Swatch watch?

One One was a race horse, One Two was one too; One One won one race, One Two won one too!

Fuzzy Wuzzy was a bear
Fuzzy Wuzzy had no hair
If Fuzzy Wuzzy had no hair
then Fuzzy Wuzzy wasn't fuzzy,
was he?

I slit a sheet, a sheet I slit,
Upon a slitted sheet I sit.
Whoever slit this sheet was a good sheet slitter.

Betty Botter bought some butter but she said the butter's bitter. If I put it in my batter it will make my batter bitter. So she bought some better butter, better than the bitter butter and put it in her batter and her batter was not bitter. So 'twas good that Betty Botter bought some better butter.

"*th*"

Theophilus Thistle, the Thistle Sifter,
Sifted a sieve of unsifted thistles.
If Theophilus Thistle, the Thistle Sifter,
Sifted a sieve of unsifted thistles,
Where is the sieve of un-sifted thistles
Theophilus Thistle, the Thistle Sifter, sifted?

I'm not a pheasant plucker,
I'm a pheasant plucker's son
I'm only plucking pheasants
'till the pheasant plucker comes.

The whiskey mixer mixes whiskey
with the whiskey mixer... *Try that one really fast!*

V

What **Hermann the German** says...

I ~~am~~ born in Berlin. →

I've lived in Hamburg ~~since~~ four years.

My neighbours are ~~sympathetic persons~~.

Somtimes we ~~are socialising~~ together.

~~On~~ one party I asked my neighbour Anna to dance.

We ~~have danced and talked~~ all night long.

She said that ~~my new shirt pleased her~~.

I ~~was really liking~~ Anna a lot.

~~In the last time~~ we have become close.

Last summer we ~~have visited~~ her parents.

For her birthday - I ~~buyed~~ her a ring.

We ~~get~~ married next year!

What **Hermann the German** should say...

I *was* born in Berlin.

I've lived in Hamburg *for* four years.

My neighbours are *likeable people.*

Somtimes we *socialise* together.

At one party I asked my neighbour Anna to dance.

We *danced and talked* all night long.

She said that *she liked my new shirt.*

I *really liked* Anna a lot.

Over the last while we have become close.

Last summer *we visted* her parents.

For her birthday - I *bought* her a ring.

We *are going to get* married next year!

Final Quiz

Part One - Words

Can you remember what these words are in English?

1. Ausnahmen ....

2. spazieren gehen ....

3. wie bereits erwähnt ....

4. übrigens ....

5. Herausforderung ....

6. dringend ....

7. Filiale ....

8. Viel Spaß! ....

Answers: 1. exceptions, 2. take a stroll,
3. as previously mentioned, 4. by the way / incidentally,
5. challenge, 6. urgent, 7. subsidiary, 8. have fun!

Part Two - Structure

1. Sometimes I ……….…. English.

   a. am speaking   *b. speak*

2. Usually I only ………………. in German.

   a. write   *b. am writing*

3. Recently I ………………….. English.

   a. didn't speak   *b. haven't spoken*

4. 2 years ago I …………... England for a week.

   a. was in   *b. have been to*

5. If I go back to England, I ………. longer.

   a. stay   *b. will stay*

6. If the weather is ……... - I'll go to Wimbledon.

   a. well   *b. good*

7. If an Irishman won Wimbledon - Ireland ...…… party for a week!

   a. will   *b. would*

8. If Ireland ………. for a week - sea levels would rise.

   a. party   *b. partied*

9. In the future communication in English .... help enhance world unity.

   a. will   *b. is going to*

10. In the future Germans will have ……... with English.

    a. trouble   *b. fun*

Answers: 1. b, 2. b, 3. b. 4. a, 5. b, 6. b, 7. b, 8. b,
9. a (prediction) *or* b (fact), 10. a *or* b - you decide...

Part Three – Wedding Plans

Hermann needs help helping Anna...

Hermann is trying to help Anna to write to her English cousins. Can you help him to correct her mistakes...

1. The wedding is going to be ~~at~~ 21st August. ....

2. We ~~invite~~ only family and friends. ....

3. ~~We will be 60 people.~~ ....

4. The whole wedding is going to be ~~in~~ a boat. ....

5. A band is going to play ~~life~~ music. ....

6. We want ~~that everyone has~~ fun! ....

Answers: 1. on... 2. are inviting... 3. There will be 60 of us.
4. on.... 5. live... 6. everyone to have *fun!*

P.S. Hermann the German and his wife lived happily ever after.

Resources

Now, you might like to get proactive by exploring online. Listening to podcasts is a great way to keep in touch with English. In particular the BBC podcasts are ideal:

www.bbc.co.uk/podcasts

You might also like to check out these news sites:

bbcnews.com	BBC News online
ft.com	The Financial Times
guardian.co.uk	The Guardian
nytimes.com	The New York Times
newsweek.com	Newsweek Magazine
time.com	Time Magazine

Most of these web sites also have video and audio options that you might find enjoyable.

The following sites may be helpful for practice:

bbclearningenglish.com

learnenglish.org.uk

englisch-hilfen.de

These sites can help you translate (*be careful!*):

leo.org   translate.google.com

These books are ideal for improving your skills:

"English Grammar In Use" by Raymond Murphy

"Business Grammar Builder" by Paul Emmerson

And this is a funny look at all the "bad" words:

"English as a Foreign F*cking Language" by Sterling Johnson

Last but not least, you could also check out this web site for further tips, hints and links:

EnglishfuerGermans.de

Glossary

Acknowledgements (Danksagung)

'English für Germans' is dedicated to the memory of my good friend Gordon S. C. McMahon (1942-2011). This book really would not have been completed without the help, support and encouragement of lots of people. First and foremost thanks to Tania for all the things that I cannot put into words. And thanks to my Mum for being so cool. Thanks to all of my family and friends (you know who you are). Thanks to all of my fellow English teachers, particularly Amanda Habbershaw (for teaching me so much) and all of my language-teaching colleagues in Karlsruhe, especially Beatriz Tapia-Adler, Véronique Rigaud-Költzsch, Amanda Kahrsch, and Gerard Taylor. "Cheers!" (Sláinte) to all at Flynn's Inn and Scruffy's Irish Pubs in Karlsruhe. A large "Nice one!" to Petra Junkert for helping me with "nuances", Lutz Kiefer for the insight into the German mindset, and Emily Curley for helping me see that I could be an English teacher - many moons ago. Thanks to Jürgen Götz and Jochen Neuber for all their friendly feedback. Special thanks to Ingrid Völker and Günther Wagner for their help fine-tuning the text. I'd also like to thank the best teacher I've ever had: Liam Tyers. Most of all I would like to thank all the students I've taught - I've learned a lot from you (even if it should be the other way around)! And last but not least, this book is dedicated to anyone who's tried teaching English to Germans! Oh, and if you have read this far - thanks to you too!

Coming next...

www.EnglishfuerGermans.de

Simon Geraghty
is an Irishman who
lives and works in Germany.
He studied Visual Communication
at the Dublin Institute of Technology
and is lecturer for Cross Media and English
at Akademie der media in Stuttgart, Germany.

NOTES

NOTES

www.ingramcontent.com/pod-product-compliance
Ingram Content Group UK Ltd.
Pitfield, Milton Keynes, MK11 3LW, UK
UKHW020222250726
13967UKWH00001B/133

9 781447 874768